Alcyone Rising:
The Path of the Awakened Feminine

KATELYN MARIAH MA, BFA

DEDICATION

This book and meditation deck are dedicated to all women who want to step into their awakened feminine and help anchor it onto the planet. It is also dedicated to all men who want to awaken their divine feminine to support balance between men and women. We are in this together. Let's change the planet!

CONTENTS

ACKNOWLEDGMENTS

I want to acknowledge all women who have been
pioneers on the path of the Awakened Feminine as I
have been since for the past 25+ years.
I want to acknowledge all the women who have been
exploring the Divine Feminine for many years and
those who are new to the path. I also want to
acknowledge the men who are working to bring
balance to their Divine Feminine nature as well.

Introduction

Welcome Beautiful Beings,

This Book and Meditation Deck are an invitation to explore the path of the Awakened Feminine, which is the human expression of the Divine Feminine. The ultimate goal is for each of us, female and male find balance within of both masculine and feminine. We need to understand the masculine and feminine individually first. The goal of this book is to share what I have learned about the feminine through my own journey.

It is imperative that all of us, women and men, discover and activate our Divine Feminine during these challenging times. The Awakened Feminine is activated through the heart so it requires us to open our hearts by exploring and releasing our old heart breaks.

Coming into alignment with the Divine Feminine within us is not about conforming to an archetypal idea of what it is but discovering how it expresses uniquely through each of us. The Divine Feminine is not about a list of qualities. It is a composite of frequency quotes that are not expressed through words.

This work comes out of Katelyn's 25+ year journey with the Divine Feminine through self-exploration and painting. The Awakened Feminine is the empowered feminine. I am focused on the energy of the Feminine, not to the exclusion of the Masculine, because they are both equally important, but at this time on the planet the feminine in both men and women has been stifled. I am female and very in touch with my feminine energy having come in with an extremely high dose of it to be an anchor for the Awakened Feminine.

Being drawn to this work says you are ready to explore it and embrace it yourself.

Here is the truth as I see it as a woman on the planet right now. This isn't about being victims or one gender having it worse than the other. Every man and woman alive today have been hijacked by the patriarchy. We all come into the world and learned to live based on a patriarchal program. We didn't choose this; we were spoon fed the program as children. Men learned how to be men and women learned to be women. We learned from wounded men and women.

My best guess, in speaking to men that I know is that it isn't easy being a man either. Each gender tends to hold the other hostage to the old stereotypes so they both stay stuck. We are all trying to find balance between the masculine and feminine energy in a time when there aren't a lot of role models. Women have been struggling for equal rights since the sixties. It hasn't been easy being a woman and we should be celebrated.

We (men and women) need to cheer each other on for being on the planet at this time. It's hard for all of us! We are here to bring back balance between the masculine and feminine, not to hold the old paradigm in place by believing and responding to the old stereotypes. My focus here is the awakening of the Divine Feminine within each of us. This is valuable work for both men and women.

The Dalai Lama said the world would be saved by the western women. I think it will be saved by men and women coming together in wholeness as the Awakened Feminine and Awakened Masculine. It is caused to celebrate that many of us are doing the deep work to bring back balance.

I bring this forward now to be a catalyst to rebalancing Feminine and Masculine energy on planet earth. This has been my sacred calling for 25+ years in this lifetime. We are entering a time of Masculine and Feminine balance because it is necessary to our evolution yet most of us don't know what that means. I am addressing the

Feminine aspect of that balance so you can learn how to bring it back into its natural harmony. It is the harmony between the Feminine and Masculine that will change life on the planet in a positive way.

There is a whole system of teachings about what it means to be in the empowered feminine. Prophets and avatars knew that the teachings would have to be hidden in order to protect them. It would be period of 13,000-26,000 years before they could be revealed. They knew that one day the cycle of protection would end, and the teachings would once again emerge and call to all women because the human race would require it to continue.

You are about to embark on an important journey, one that will take you into the authentic mystery of the Divine Feminine, which is an aspect that is in all of us. The feminine power that was hidden for so long is now revealed. This is not to say that we become the Goddess but that we embrace the Divine Feminine as it expresses through our human and spiritual nature.

This feminine wisdom is rooted in the Ancient Heart of the Divine Feminine and brought through the lineage of the Divine Mother, through Venus, the Pleiades, through Lemuria, to Egypt and to Katelyn Mariah. Katelyn has higher consciousness connections to these four places. Lemuria was a seed culture from many other civilizations. Each soul that enters the planet Earth is said to enter through the Pleiades.

Lemuria was an ancient civilization which existed before and during the time of Atlantis. It is believed to have been in the South Pacific between North America and Australia. At the peak of the civilization, Lemurians were both highly evolved and very spiritual.

Venusians are extraterrestrial beings who originated on in higher realms of Venus. Venusians are happy, joyous and highly spiritual, heart- based beings. They also hold a lot of feminine energy.

The inhabitants of Pleiades, known as Pleiadean's, are a highly evolved humanoid race and the next step in our evolution. It is said that Pleiadean's are here to help us in our spiritual journey to enlightenment. Cherokee legend states that their people originated in the Pleiades and they came to this world as star seeds of light and knowledge. The Pleiadean's are of a fifth dimensional frequency, which is one of love and creativity in a Goddess Society. As part of the Taurus constellation they hold more feminine energy.

Women in ancient Egypt were ahead of their time. They could not only rule the country, but also had many of the same basic human rights as men. One of the first women to hold the rank of pharaoh was Hatshepsut, who began her rule in about 1,500 B.C.E. Hatshepsut took care of her people and built temples to the gods as well as other public buildings.

Egypt treated its women better than any of the other major civilizations of the ancient world. The Egyptians believed that joy and happiness were legitimate goals of life and regarded home and family as the major source of delight.

Women held many important and influential positions in Ancient Egypt and typically enjoyed many of the legal and economic rights given to the men within their respective social class.

Why Alcyone Rising?

Alcyone is a stellar being, from the constellation Pleiades also known as the Seven Stars or Seven Sisters. Alcyone is known as the Central One because she is the largest star in the Pleiades. She has a special frequency that she vibrates into the universe. The Seven Sisters are found on the shoulder blade of the constellation of Taurus the Bull. Each of the stars in the cluster of Pleiades are within one degree of each other.

In Greek mythology Alcyone was a queen, the daughter of King Aeolus, the guardian of the winds. Many ancient traditions believed that Alcyone was the Spiritual Central

Sun, the Mother Sun that emits creative light to the planet. As the Mother Sun she carries high feminine energy. She bestows intelligence of intuition to seekers at a high level of consciousness and knowledge, helping the seeker grow to be conscious of the Divine Wisdom and Knowledge. It is said that the Pleiades was originally created through sound and vibration. Alcyone, the brightest star in the system is over 800 times more luminous than our Sun.

The Pleiades are featured in the star-lore of many ancient cultures. For example, at Lascaux in central France, a cave painting from 16,500 years ago shows the Pleiades in their usual place in the constellation of Taurus.

It is obvious from legends and myths that the Pleiadean Star System was the locus of our cosmic inheritance and the source of mystical wisdom known by the High Initiates of the Mystery Schools of Isis. Alcyone carries the energy of the divine feminine mysteries.

And all of this delicious feminine energy is rising again from the stellar being of Alcyone and available to all of us!

Our Matriarchal Female Ancestors

Our Matriarchal female ancestors had access to a kind of spiritual power and clairvoyance, within her soul, that was very powerful making women natural oracles. Their gift of imagination, which was in unity with nature, became the basis for higher development of the life of ideas. They brought the forces of nature into themselves, where they integrated into the soul. This created the seeds of memory, which would be passed. Because of their deep connection with nature, women could interpret the signs that were found there, and people came to them to translate the signs they were seeing in nature. Early societies considered the ability of reproduction, a co-creative ability, which women shared with the Creator. This ability was considered the highest endorsement the Creator can bestow on his much-loved souls and it was gifted to women. As a result, women received the greatest respect within the community because it was through them that human existence on the planet continued. The gift of birthing has been minimized and taken for granted for the last 2000 years as if it were no big deal. Women need to get back to being respected for the ability to create life. It is a BIG DEAL, to bring a being into this world through your body. It is time to venerate this gift!

As women we have been living under the shadow of the women in our bloodline, LONG ENOUGH! It's time to transform and transmute the energy of the oppressed women archetype carried by our female ancestors. It is time to unplug from the patriarchy. It is time for women to throw off the shackles we have dutifully worn for thousands of years and step onto the Path of the Awakened Feminine. Woman are all initiates of the New

Feminine way.

At the Peace Conference in Canada in 2009, The Dalia Lama said" The world will be saved by the Western Woman." I feel that this was a call to action for women throughout the west and the world. Before we can impact our sisters, brothers and the world, we must make the journey within to find the ancient wisdom of the Feminine in ourselves and bring it into the world. As we dive for the pearls that are within us and embody them so we can impart this wisdom to our daughters, granddaughters, sisters and friends.

The Path of the Awakened Feminine is an initiation into the new way for women to be in the world, to embrace their true and authentic power and spirit so we can share the gifts that only we, has women have.

I believe empowered, Authentic Women connected to the Awakened Feminine and Awakened Men will save the world.

No one would refute the fact that women have been oppressed for thousands of years and still are on some levels. If you explore the archetype of Woman you find oppression all the way back to Adam and Eve.

The Myth of Lilith

In the original creation story, Adam and Lilith were the first people created. They were created at the same time as equals. Some believe that they were created as one being that was later split into two beings. Lilith was the natural Awakened Feminine principle and Adam with the natural Awakened Masculine principle

Lilith represented the wild feminine because she operated from her instincts, knowing what she wanted and needed. She was authentic and chose to live in integrity and to make her own choices about life.

She didn't want to be subservient to Adam, she was his equal. She left the Garden when Adam insisted that she follow his rules and refused to obey the angel's command to return. She was punished for stepping out and being her authentic self and women have been living under this suppression for 6000 years. Now we all carry the archetypes of the Awakened Feminine, Lilith, and the Suppressed Feminine, Eve, in our DNA and they are in conflict with one another.

Lilith has been demonized through history and is seen as a temptress or evil woman. Her shadow side has been exaggerated. She is said to prey on men sexually and kill new-born babies.

What a story to keep the natural feminine at bay! When we go back to the origin of Lilith we find that she represents the natural feminine instincts and that is the Lilith that I want to shine a light on rather than the story of her being banished to the underworld, in our story Lilith went off to a cave to live in an authentic feminine way…

The frequency codes of the Divine Feminine are the original structure of women, when they were seeded onto the planet, as they were manifest in the being of Lilith. They were not the qualities of Eve, who was subservient to men as described in the Bible but were more like Lilith who had all of the qualities we will discover on the Path of the Awakened Feminine.

The pushing down and subjugating of women started way back to the Adam and Eve mythology, where Adam was made to be higher and more powerful than Eve.

They were not seen as equals. This story is the seed program used to disempower women.

It is said that Lilith was then banished and rejected by God after it was found that she was stronger and more intelligent that Adam and she would not obey the commands of Adam. Lilith to me, was the first Women's Liber. Even if it is just a story, that mythology permeates the female archetype because it has been passed down from generation to generation. The history of women's oppression would fill many books, so I won't dwell on it. We can just agree that women have been oppressed in many ways going way back in time.

This energy of the Feminine has been protected by the Lemurian, Pleiadean, Venusian and Egyptian lineages so it could return in its pure form. This is a Divine Energy that is a part of us all, both women and men.

This isn't a book about women's is about woman's empowerment and reclaiming our powerful, innate Feminine wisdom. It is about activating the Path of the New Feminine within you so it can express in a unique way in the world.

Sit back for a moment and let me tell you a story...

In the Beginning...

According to the original story, Lilith was thrown out of the Garden. Where did she go, you might ask? She retreated alone to the Crystal Womb and waited for other women to join her. While she waited, she maintained the Awakened Feminine frequencies in her expression. The women who joined her came from Venus, Pleiades, Lemuria and ancient Egypt, all of the places where empowered women resided. These women were in touch with what it meant to be in their authentic feminine power and presence. The Crystalline Womb has been the sacred vessel holding the technology of the Awakened Feminine and the power of the feminine has grown in strength as it has been nurtured and held there for thousands of years. It is called the Awakened Feminine because it is a hybrid of the Ancient Feminine.

The women designated to carry the Awakened Feminine template in all of her power finally retreated off planet to the Crystal Womb. They have been in training in a mystery school for thousands of years. The teachings you hold in your hands are to help you remember your feminine power and awaken your authentic self which is the Awakened Feminine.

The Crystal Womb

Very few people knew where the Crystal Womb was hidden. Only women who were selected through a special process could go there. Its location wasn't share in order to protect this precious technology.

Imagine a crystal space that looks like a womb, embedded in a cave in a far-away mountain in another space and time. Inside the cave are 63 large crystals, some hanging from the ceiling of the cave and some rising from the floor. The crystals are Lemurian crystals and they were created to hold and store information for long periods of time. The crystalline structure was programmed with a frequency code of the Awakened Feminine by a woman that held that quality in her personal technology. The women lived in the Crystal Womb caretaking the crystals and preserving the 63 frequency codes.

As their time as caretaker was ending, they took on female apprentices and taught them the technologies within the crystals so they could take over maintaining the crystal field. The apprentices were taught to live in the Way of the Awakened Feminine was a heart centered way of life. There were always 7 women at a time, each of them caretaking and amplifying 9 frequency codes. This procession of women happened over and over again for thousands of years. Imagine the power that has building up because of this process. In order to be a crystal caretaker each woman had to go through a long initiation so they could hold the Awakened Feminine Frequency codes within their body.

They originally came from the Pleiades and represented the 7 Sisters, Alcyone, Maia, Asterope, Celaeno, Taygete, Electra and Merope. These 7 Sisters hold the energy of community and the Divine Feminine in harmony not only with each other but with the Divine Masculine. Alcyone means "The Central One and according to the story Alcyone was a priestess at Argos. Now that I am sharing this story, I can tell you that the Crystal Womb was on Alcyone and that is where this sacred wisdom was held all of these years, thus the name Alcyone Rising. Through thousands of years initiates came from Venus, Lemuria, The Pleiades and Egypt as well so you have the four-fold nature of the Awakened Feminine.

The 7 Sisters are ready to release this ancient feminine wisdom to the world and have asked me to share it with all of my sisters on the planet.

Working with this ancient yet new wisdom:

- Will help the seeker become consciously aware of the Divine Feminine knowledge and wisdom.

- Will transform old patterns and initiate new ones

- Will Immerse you in a sacred womb of wisdom of the Divine Feminine

- Serves to stimulate and awaken the heart center

- Liberates the higher level of intuition and creative intelligence

- Raise your consciousness to 5D

- Will help bring back the balance of Feminine and Masculine energy in you and to all humans on planet earth.

- As an initiate of this work you will touch others and help spread this new consciousness

Working with the Awakened Feminine frequency codes

will open higher levels of consciousness in seekers, unfolding within them the potentials and gifts that are inherent and manifest on the higher planes of being. This will expand heart intelligence and put you in touch with the innate gifts that you are here to share. Each one of us is here to play a part that only we can play in the evolution of the planet at this time. It is imperative that we shed the layers of the oppressed feminine, awaken our heart once again and don the robe of the Awakened Feminine. In doing so we are awakening our Heart space where we can live from love.

An awakened heart is the doorway to the Divine Feminine and Divine Masculine.

Alcyone Rising is your invitation to step into your deep Feminine and help heal our collective wounds as women. As we step into our power, we empower all women on the planet, by knowing who we are, knowing our value, and our worth intrinsically in every cell and in every breath. By doing this we are uplifting our sisters on the path who may still feel oppressed and separate. We are embracing our deep feminine nature and claiming our

right to be here and I, Katelyn Mariah and the keepers of
this ancient wisdom are here to support you on the
journey.

So, what is in the way of women fully embodying their
Awakened Feminine? I believe it is the mother wound.
The deep wound that spans generations of women back
in time through our personal and collective lineage.

ALCYONE RISING

The Mother Wound:

We need to explore the mother wound because of the power it has on women and how they move through the world. The mother wound is a direct result of women's oppression. This shadow aspect is why we have developed limiting beliefs about ourselves.

We have lost our wild nature because of the mother wound. What many women don't realize is that the core issue at the center of women's empowerment is the mother wound, which is part of the feminine collective story. For women, this is our original heart break. It was the beginning of our descent to close the doors of our hearts. It makes me wonder if this is why so many women are having and dying from heart attacks. We are all walking around with broken hearts!! Every woman I talk to says they have issues with their mother. So, what do we do about it?

Mothers play a crucial role in her daughter's early development and throughout life. Ironically most mothers never learned how to love well because they learned from wounded mothers. Even the best-intentioned mothers are often living from an unhealed heart, resulting in most girls growing up with unhealed wounds which they bring into this core mother/daughter relationship. Even as adults this wound colors how women see themselves and approach life. Tragically, this often creates a cycle that repeats itself through multiple generations, which not only belong to us, but to our mothers, grandmothers, great grandmothers and beyond. And until it is healed, we pass it to our daughters. These emotional responses are recorded and trapped in our DNA. This cellular memory is hard to retrieve, especially if it isn't from our own personal experience. What happened to our ancestors has become part of our story and we don't even know it is there or what it is.

For women who are adopted the mother wound is compounded. They spend a lot of their life trying to find their worthiness because they feel abandoned and rejected. Add to this the bloodline wound and the collective wound and you have a deep wound to heal.

The mother wound is an archetype we all carry and have probably carried through many lifetimes. The mother wound is the pain of being a woman, in a society dominated and control by men. This wound is passed down through the generations of women around the world. It is in our bloodline and in our cellular memory and both are hard to access.

It originated when the patriarchy became the dominate force on the planet and the matriarchy all but disappeared. Patriarchy is a social system in which the father or eldest male heads the family. Men hold the power and women are largely excluded. Decisions are made based on patriarchal lines.

The matriarchy was a social system in which females held primary power. Women were the political leaders and had social privilege and were the property owners. Both of these systems were unbalanced. We have been under the influence of the Patriarchy for a few thousand years, so our female ancestors have been impacted by it. This means there is a lot of oppression and male dominance for women to heal. We need a balance of both masculine and feminine power to shift this paradigm.

The mother wound is passed down at a preconscious level as the infant absorbs the stress hormones of the mother while we are nestled in physical unity deep inside the womb. The baby is absorbing the pain, fear, anger, frustration and grief that grows in a woman when she tries to explore and understand her power and potential in a society that doesn't support it. This forces the baby to internalize the dysfunctional coping mechanisms learned by previous generations of women, passed down to their daughters.

In my mother's generation women clearly had no power.

This played out in my family by my mother giving power and privilege to my brothers while my sister and I were essentially invisible. My mother bought into the idea that women had no value and passed it unknowingly to her daughters like her mother did before her. She still refers to herself as a "commoner". I didn't buy into it, but it still influenced me. With years of personal work, I have broken the chain for my daughter, my granddaughter and future generations of women in my line.

The feminine voice, beliefs and practices have suffered under the patriarchy. She has lost her value and significance and had been censored, ridiculed and denied a voice. The Feminine has been put down for its wisdom, intuitive vision, beliefs and intelligence. Women have been forced to become more masculine to fit in and compete. Women have been dis-credited for expressing emotions in the world. How many times did you hear "you are too emotional or too sensitive"? I know I heard it often.

Women have been fighting for equal treatment for 50 years and it still feels like she has made little headway in getting equal rights. Women around the world have experienced brutal treatment in the form of torture, abuse, rape, being objectified, sexualized, diminished and harmed. Our female ancestors were burnt at the stake and drowned as witches and these energies still pulse through our blood. Through it all we were expected to be silent. The female blood line is loaded with debris and that needs to be cleared.

Only recently through the #MeToo movement have the abuses women have suffered been brought to light. Still some of the women who have reported abuse by men in power have had their validity questioned and have been ridiculed. Our own president, who should be a role model, is modeling behavior that perpetuates the abuse and denigration of women. This has set a precedent to keep the abuse going.

This inequality is reaffirmed through social and psychological archetypes and stereotypes through the media, in our communities, in our families and everywhere. Women are expected to look good, care for their families, work full time and smile through it all and be superhuman. You might think those are just stereotypes but they are still alive today, impacting women.

My own mother had an unspoken belief that men had more value than women and my sister and I both understood that by her actions toward them and us. I am sure it came out of her own lack of feeling valued which came down through her bloodline. Whether we as women heard it said out loud or not, we could feel in the fiber of society that we didn't have to same value as our male counterparts. In the past 40-50 years, we have made headway toward equality, but we have a long way to go and nothing will really change until we individually and collectively heal the mother wound.

The mother wound expresses itself through these dysfunctional coping mechanisms which are used to unconsciously process the pain:

- Comparison: Which is over-compensation for not feeling good enough

- Shame: Always in the background where we feel that there is something wrong with us. Shame is often a natural response for women. It is an overpowering physical feeling that makes us respond automatically. Most of the time it causes us to back off.

- Attenuation: Feeling you must remain small to be loved. If you somehow shine and share your gifts people will be jealous and not like you. Authenticity still creates distance because it isn't socially accepted. I feel that when I express authentically.

- Persistent sense of guilt for wanting to have more than you currently have, as though you don't deserve it. Guilt is a big one for women.

- Internalization: We make what is happening outside of us our fault and feel like we aren't good enough, don't have value, are wrong and we abandon ourselves. This happens a lot in our interactions with men.

From those mechanisms which are mostly unconscious, the mother wound manifests in the following ways:

- Co-dependency and people pleasing

- A distorted self-image and not knowing who you are

- Body image issues, like seeing yourself as fat when you are not.

- An inability to be authentic because you feel it will threaten others

- Self-sabotage and relationship sabotage

- Acquiescing to men

- Minimizing your gifts and talents as if they are no big deal.

- Having a high tolerance for poor treatment from others, especially from men

- Feeling competitive with other women, for the job, the man, the opportunity, the friend. Women we must get beyond this!

- Jealousy, cattiness and gossip

- Being overly rigid and controlling

- One-upmanship

- Self-abandonment and rejection. Rejecting parts of us that feel inadequate

- Eating disorders, depression, anxiety and addictive behaviors

- Body shaming ourselves and other women

- Sadly, many women have become masculinized to be seen and valued in our society and divorcing themselves completely from the feminine. This was the only way to get a good job.

- Over-compensation to look good, feel you are okay and fit in.

- We fall for societies standard for what women should look like and act like.

- Ghosting relationships, which means stop interacting without explanation or discussion.

All of this has given us good reason to close off our hearts, but our hearts are saying NO MORE!! It is time to heal this ancient wound and remove it from our consciousness not just for ourselves but for our mothers, grandmothers, daughters, sisters and granddaughters. It's time to heal our hearts, so we can stand in our authentic power! The mother wound is one of the most complex obstacles women face because it is so deep, so entrenched and unconscious. One issue can weave into another, so it is hard to sort out or even see. It has been a part of women's psyche for so long that it is automatic.

This wound keeps us from our power and is the cause of our broken hearts. It is time to become fearless and as big, authentic, creative and successful as we can!

We need to remember our mothers have their own mother wound. It is important to remember that our mothers are someone else's daughter and they were someone's daughter too and all of them carried the wound. My mother's mother was not warm, nurturing, understanding or compassionate. She was 16 when she married a 60-year-old man, my grandfather. Talk about deep wounding. She must have thought that finding a father would heal the wound she didn't even know she had. She called him "Daddy" until the day she died. He didn't like women and was vocal about it in the senate. He was a powerful man, a State Senator, so maybe that made her feel more powerful too.

How was she or my mother who learned from her, going to be loving and nurturing to me? That wasn't active in our bloodline, shame, feeling inadequate and comparison were. My mother was not taught the art of mothering. Somehow, I figured out how to do it for my own children, even though I made mistakes. My grandmother, my mother, my sister, me and my daughter are all products of our legacy. I want that to change for my granddaughter, Opal.

The core part of healing the mother wound is reconnecting with our sisterhood, The Divine Feminine and our earth mother, Gaia. Women have internalized the patriarchal truths and tenants into our bodies and that is why women treat each other the way they do. It's time to release this program which is deep in our cells. We do this by validating and feeling our experience and releasing it to heal. The Goddess wants to evolve along with us as we become the Awakened Feminine.

We can't save our mothers, yet to heal our own wound we must set our mothers free, offering compassion, forgiveness and understanding because we understand our shared legacy. It wasn't their fault, just as it isn't ours. A whole book could be written on how to heal the mother wound but I will give a few suggests getting your started and encourage you to do deeper exploration on this issue

- Make a list of things you felt like you didn't get from your mother, emotionally, physically and spiritually and do them for yourself. This can take a period of time, but it will be worth it. Choose something from your list once a week and work with it until you have gone through all of them. Go through them again and again until you feel complete.

- Look at the list I created about ways we compensate and pick out the ones that fit for you. Take one a month and explore how it impacts your life and how you can change the behavior. Practice new ways to respond. Soon they will become second nature.

- Find a great therapist, hypnotherapist, body worker or energy worker and start working on this issue with her. This will help your release issues you can't get to on your own. Katelyn is available to do this work with you individually as well.

- Find a photo that you like of you as a child and put her in your sacred space or in a frame on your dresser, so you can see it every day. Look at her and speak to her every day in nurturing ways. Let her know you love her.

- Let your human mother off the hook. Find a way to forgive her and realize that she is just a reflection of a deeper issue. She did the best coming from her own mother wound and most likely didn't have the resources you had to confront and heal the issues.

- Be conscious of the self-talk you pass to your daughters and what you say to yourself. Stop it before you get pulled into a loop that you don't want to go into.

- Find ways to support your daughters as they develop and understand their power and potential.

- Be gentle with yourself as you go through this process of clearing and integration.

- Do a personal exploration of the Goddess/Divine Feminine Movement

- Read Women Who Run with the Wolves by Dr. Clarissa Pinkola Estes and A Woman's Worth by Marianne Williamson

- Find ways to fall in love with you!!!

- Love yourself fiercely!

On a personal level, the mother wound is an opportunity for healing and for transformation. Transformation doesn't imply removing or fixing the traumas and scars from childhood that we all carry. It is about slowly developing a new relationship with what is difficult in your life so that it is no longer a controlling factor. It's time to initiate and support each of our sisters into their full power. It's time to re-establish sisterhood again. As women friends, we need to find ways to support each other through the messiness of changing and transforming.

After the second heart attack (I had five + open heart surgery) a group of girlfriends gathered to celebrate the fact that I was still alive. Two of my girlfriends organized and planned it and there were 15 of us including my sister and my daughter. I hand-picked each woman based on how I felt they had been a part in my healing process. My friend Linda and I were talking one day before the party and she said is there anything special you would like? I couldn't think of anything because I thought the whole idea was special enough, so I flippantly said I wanted a crown. One of my friends had a special ritual crown that was made for healing work that she does, and she brought it with her. She didn't know that was my only request so that made it even more special. I got to wear it for the day after she ceremoniously placed it on my head.

We had a meal together and then we all sat in a circle and drummed just like women did in the past. We went around the circle and each of my friends told me what I meant to them. I had never experienced anything like this, and it shocked me in a good way to hear what they said. I was hearing things about myself that I didn't think people noticed and things that I hadn't thought were any big deal. It was so healing for my heart. This was a step in healing the mother wound for all of us just by acknowledging the beauty in a sister. Every woman should experience this, and we need to hold Individual Awakening Feminine circles like this for each other to continue healing the mother wound.

We need to remember someone else's success is not our failure. We are all unique and have something to share with the world that only we can share. I love the idea of cheering each other on so we can all live authentic, prosperous, healthy lives.

Now that you know about and have explored the mother wound, we can put that aside and start to explore The Path of the Awakened Feminine. By allowing ourselves to explore the many facets of The Path of The Awakened Woman we can birth ourselves into our true identity, which is our own unique expression that no one can take from us. The world needs each and every one of us to impact change.

ALCYONE RISING

Why Katelyn Mariah?

Why would this come through Katelyn Mariah at this time? As a point of reference Katelyn started on the Path of the Awakened Feminine in 1995 when images of the Goddess started streaming through her in a visionary manner. Over a period of 6 weeks to 2 months Katelyn was able to capture 44 of these images which later became a meditation deck called "Awakening the Goddess Meditation Deck". Women around the world still work with this deck today.

Katelyn also came onto the planet with an extreme

amount of feminine energy. She has taken the MMPI, a personality test, two times and each time she scored off the charts in the Feminine on the Masculine/Feminine scale. She was told that her score fell into a range that isn't even on the charts.

A reflection about Katelyn's art by the late Ron Mangravite

This is a quote from Ron Mangravite, a mystic and mystery school facilitator, and expert on mythology and symbolism who was fascinated by Katelyn's paintings.

"In attempting to find her identity, which is the Goddess, and find ways she could manifest, she apparently went down deep enough to get totally past Katelyn, to get totally past everything but her femininity, because these images are the Goddess.

Katelyn dug down deep enough to get past anything that is the person and found real legitimate expressions that came from such a mixed bag of a culture that it would be very difficult for her to have truly cheated. She does not know that some of these symbols are Babylonian, Sumerian, Chinese, and Welsh. She could not possibly have known without at least 10 or 15 years of study. She could not have made this mixed bag up by faking it. It has to come from someplace very real.

And therefore, I am extremely privileged to be here to be more or less, the official midwife to announce to the world that this is not just an artist - Katelyn is an initiate of consciousness."

Katelyn believes that she brought these frequency codes of the Feminine through and it took her 25+ years to integrate them in herself. As a visionary artist Katelyn's art is prophetic so much of what she paints speaks about something in the future. That was true of the Awaken the Goddess meditation cards. Katelyn went through her final initiation from March 20,2016-March 2019, through the deep, transformational opening of her heart on the physical, spiritual and emotional levels. During that time period she had 5 heart attacks and open-heart surgery. Simultaneously she experienced a deep purging of issues that were overlaid on her authentic feminine expression.

As a result, this information started flowing through her and on to these pages, as did new images of the Awakened Feminine.

Katelyn has chosen 63 of her paintings to represent the frequency codes of the Awakened Feminine. The images in this deck span those 25+ years of Katelyn's Journey exploring the Awakened Feminine. They were painted at various times through-out the process that is why they are all so different.

Learn more about Katelyn's heart initiation in her book (Resilient Heart: a holistic guide to having a healthy heart, available at Mystick Creek Publishing) and her art at Katelyn Mariah Visionary Artist.

<u>The meditation deck that goes with this book</u> is ordered separately unless you have purchased it directly from Katelyn Mariah. It is available at www.MystickCreekPublishing.com

Let the journey to the Awakened Feminine begin...

This book and deck of images is about taking back our power so you can live as Empowered, Authentic women again. It will take you on a journey of self-discovery that will change your life.

Women are remembering as a collective. The call of the Divine Feminine beckons to your heart. Your heart aches with a deep longing for confirmation of what you feel inside of you. There are parts and pieces of you that have been forgotten and are now being remembered. There are hidden wisdom and skills rising in you. Let's

join together to anchor our powerful Awakened
Feminine onto the planet together.

You are connecting with this wisdom

- To activate, enliven and bring forth ancient
  wisdom that is encoded in your cells.

- To access hidden skills, talents and abilities so
  you can use them in the world

- To experience a deeper connection to the cosmic
  nature of Earth and the deep feminine energy she
  holds

- To reconnect with the innate intelligence of your
  body, your inner physician, so you can return to
  and live in homeostasis

- To connect with the Intelligence of your heart.

As the feminine, Lemurian, Venusian, Pleiadean,
Egyptian memory is activated in you, it will become the

base of your own spiritual and inner wisdom and will find unique expression through you in the world. These basic beliefs where built on a foundation of belief in a higher power, in love and in respect for each other and the love and respect of the earth. All life was harmonious, heart centered and united originally. We are bringing that balance and harmony back.

We are the dreamers and we are awakening now!

ALCYONE RISING

Who is the Awakened Feminine?

The Awakened Feminine is a powerful creature who can create life, birth children from her womb and create her desires in the outer world. This is an inner technology given to every woman. This technology not only creates life but is a creative force that allows women to manifest their creations in the outer world. Woman have been distracted away from these creative gifts on purpose because it was seen as a threat. Distraction was part of the unfolding story so women would forget their power.

The Awakened Feminine is the original structure of

women when we were seeded onto the planet. It is not the frequency codes of Eve, which is the shadow feminine, but the frequency codes of Lilith. The story of Eve is part of the program to disempower women. The story of Lilith was hidden.

Lilith was the archetype of the Empowered Woman and Earth was not ready for her at that juncture in the story. Yes, she was pushed back by the patriarchy but not in a bad way as it appears. It was in the storyline of the Earth. Male dominance coupled with oppression of women. It was part of the plan. If we understand that on a higher-level, we were part of planning this creation story it takes the sting out of it and gives us power.

At this time in our history, the feminine energy/woman will return as Empowered beings to bring back the balance of the masculine and feminine for co-operative living. A balance where men and women are equal but who each bring an important piece the other doesn't have. May Alcyone Rising be your catalyst of empowerment on the New Feminine Path.

Rewilding the Awakened Feminine

I have healed the Mother Wound, now what?

Now it is time to reclaim our wild nature.

If you had a chance to leave everything you know
behind so you could step into your wild, authentic
awakened feminine self could you do it? Would you
know what to do? Would you even know what it
meant?

The wild, authentic, awakened feminine is our true
nature as women. Wild doesn't mean out of control. It
means you are in touch with your beautiful,
authentic, dancing with abandoned, dreaming,

magical, creative, life loving self. We each have that within us. Think of how you were as a child before the age of five. That is your true nature.

In Women who Run with Wolves Estes says that the nature of women is wild, natural, passionately creative, with great instincts and ageless knowing. She believes that the Wild Woman is an endangered species. Society has worked hard to tame our wild nature through domestication. Estes believes that without the Wild Women, society becomes over-domesticated, fearful, uncreative and trapped. I feel smothered just typing this.

The wild women, the ancient one, the wolf woman and the tree woman are part of our true nature. She knows who she is. She is creative, intuitive, shamanic, instinctual, sensual, earthy and endangered. Yes, endangered and it is time we save her before she goes extinct! We have had our superpowers taken away and it is time to take them back!!

To heal we must return to our wild, authentic, awakened feminine selves. Part of that is going back to our wild nature. What if the way out of domestication has to do with re-wilding our imaginations, un-domesticating our lives, and reclaiming not only our rights but also our health and well-being?

I love the idea of re-wilding our imaginations, ditching our domesticated selves and reclaiming our rights and our health. First, I like the made-up word, re-wilding and un-domesticating because they go against domestication and move toward reclaiming our wildness. This reminds me of how I was stirred and inspired in the early 90's by the Wild Woman movement started by the book "Women who Run with Wolves". I was part of a Wild Women artist group and we did a lot of wild and crazy things together. We went back to our wild nature and we didn't care what people thought. This was our way of unleashing our creative spirits and it worked! Women in our art collective created amazing art! I felt alive and free with these women.

Estes also believes that healthy wolves and healthy women share certain psychic characteristics. We are in touch with our higher senses, we are playful and imaginative. Wolves and women are relational and community oriented by nature. They know how to work together toward a common goal. Wolves and women are deeply intuitive, intensely concerned for their young, their mate and the tribe. They can adapt to change and are very brave. When we are in touch with our wild nature, we just know what to do.

The nature of our souls is the same as the nature of animals. The difference between animals and humans is intellect and the ability to think, create and problem solve and often those things get in the way.

Our wild nature is chipped away through the socialization process, what Don Miguel Ruiz, author of the Four Agreements calls domestication. We are taught to blend in with the pack. Words like "day-dreaming", are used to describe a child who is in touch with her spirit. Children are told they are imaging things when they have a "knowing" about something. These kinds of phrases chisel away at the child's ability to trust their natural instincts. Before they know it, they don't trust their intuition, knowing and dreams because adults told them it wasn't okay.

The instinctual nature of women has dropped behind the veil of the material world because of concrete, noise, stress, obligations and responsibilities and fast pace way of life, people have lost touch with their wild nature and true essence. We have been domesticated yet that doesn't mean that domestication has to be our primary mode of operation. Domestication has little to do with our authentic wild self and a lot to do with conformity and fitting in. It has little to do with what our heart and soul desires and more about being enslaved.

The Wild Woman is becoming an endangered species. How sad when it is really our true nature to be wild. The word wild congers up all kinds of images of unruly, aggressive, uncivilized behavior but it is also that which is natural and instinctual that can't and should not be tamed. To some, the wild nature might seem like shadow because it isn't the "acceptable" way to be.

What happened to our wild nature? We are born inspirited and inspired. Children gravitate toward the earth, nature and the forest when they go out to play. They play in the mud and eat flowers, jump like frogs and run like horses. They are in touch with their instincts, their imagination and intuition and their worlds are alive. Children talk to animals, to bugs, to birds and to plants because they can feel the spirit in each of them. Children are in touch with their wild nature and because we were all once children that same wild nature is available to us.

In one of my favorite children's books, Maurice Sendak tells the story of Max, who one evening plays around his home making "mischief" in a wolf costume. As punishment, his mother sends him to bed without supper. That is how we were all domesticated, we were punished for doing things that didn't fit the status quo. In his room, Max sees a mysterious, wild forest and a sea in his imagination. He sails to the land of the Wild things. The Wild Things are fearsome-looking monsters, but in his imagination, Max is fiercer and concurs the wild things by staring at them and dancing with them.

 Detached from our natural instincts, we shift our prospective away from soul on to ego and begin to live from fear rather than love. Fear restricts our energy, disconnects us from spirit and aborts the process of natural manifestation. We make decisions out of fear and the world responds back in fear. Social programming has left us over-domesticated, fearful, uncreative and trapped.

Is there hope of regaining our wild nature? We have
projected our own wounds on how we treat nature
and the earth. I think that is what we are witnessing
right now, along with a movement around the world
of people banding together to break free of it. Estes
Pinkola and Sendak were planting seeds toward this
movement and now those seeds are blossoming. We
have reached momentum and are watching it in the
freedom movements across the globe. People are so
tired of feeling fearful, un-creative and trapped, they
are willing to give their lives to change things.

We have been away from our wildish nature too long
as slaves to domestication and social programming.
Many women are turning toward their wild nature, a
few at a time and this is how we are going to reclaim
our true nature and our health. It is exciting to watch
people waking up and begin to explore the wild and
natural creature that they are. This needs to be
nurtured and supported.

The wild man and wild woman live imaginative
lives. They are not afraid to dream their dreams and
make them a reality. They are using their
imaginations and following their instinctive intuition.
It is from the place of our wild, instinctual nature that

we will be able to survive the shift of time and arrive at a new civilization. Our wild nature is real, and it is our home.

This is not an easy process because it means questioning all the things we were taught as children. It means letting go of judgment, self-censorship and comparing. It means moving toward acceptance of self and others, of saying what is on our minds and not worrying about what others think and not comparing ourselves to each other to fit in and feel accepted because that is where the creative juice and genius is. That is the edge of the norm and the beginning of new territory. That is where the gate to the playground is. From that place, we can burst forth a new world and our life, our health and our soul depend on it.

Doesn't that sound more colorful, and sexy than what we have been doing for way too long?

Finding our wild nature is an inside job that we take one step at a time. It is about reaching past our false sense of identity as a woman that is given to us by our culture. We are no longer teenage girls vying for attention from our current heart throb or cave women trying to get the guy just to survive. There is no need for judgment, jealousy or competition that we experience through the mother wound. Those days are gone.

This quote from Estes describes our innate self from my prospective:

"When women reassert their relationship with the wildish nature, they are gifted with a permanent and internal watcher, a knower, a visionary, an oracle, an inspiratrice, and intuitive, a maker, a creator, an inventor, and a listener who guides, suggests and urges vibrant life in the inner and outer world. When women are close to nature, the fact of that relationship glows through them. This wild teacher, wild mother, wild mentor supports their inner and outer lives, no matter what."

Every woman has something unique to offer the world. Finding and embracing your wild, authentic, awakened feminine nature is the beginning.

Ways to help you embody the Awakened Feminine

1. Get creative! We are natural creators. Find a creative outlet that you enjoy and work with it on a regular basis. Let your intuition guide you. Most importantly have fun and enjoy what you create without being critical of the outcome. This isn't about creating a product it is about enjoying the process. Read the book "The Artist's Way" as a way to begin a new creative process.

2. Moving your body is an amazing way to start embodying your feminine nature. Put on music that stimulates your senses and just let your body flow naturally with the rhythm. Dance as though no one is watching! Try yoga. Go for long walks in the forest.

3. Self-care is an important feminine way. Set up your bathroom like a luxurious spa, with candles, flowers and yummy essential oils. Fill up the bathtub and add your favorite bubble bath fragrance. Turn on your favorite relaxing music and sink into the bubbles and relax.

4. Practice trusting your intuition. We are taught that our intuition isn't real and that we need to follow our mind but for women, intuition is our most important guidance system. Listen to your heart. Listen to your body. Follow your instincts.

5. Explore your sensuality. This is different than your sexuality. We have five senses, smell, taste, sight, hearing and touch. Take a day to just focus on one sense at a time. Find ways to stimulate that particular sense. Make that sense the one you navigate with the majority of the day. Do this with each of the five senses.

6. Do a meditation practice where you specifically aim to connect with the Divine Feminine. You might find a guided meditation that you like or just sit quietly with the intention of connecting with the Divine Feminine. You might pick a particular Goddess to work with and get an image or statue of her to focus on.

7. Observe Nature's cycles and your own cycles. Pay attention to the moon phases and celebrate

the New and Full moon in some way. The New Moon is a time to plant seeds for what you want to create, and the Full moon is the time to harvest them. Check out ways to make a ritually and do it with each moon. Pay attention to the seasons, Summer, Fall, Winter, Spring. Honor your menstrual cycles in some way. Instead of being upset because you have your period find a way to celebrate it.

8. Dress in ways that make you happy and make you feel feminine. Nurture your inner Goddess with wonderful fabrics and lovely colors and experiment to see what you like. Find beautiful scarves that you like and wear them. Totally change your wardrobe to make you feel beautiful.

9. Work with crystals that will help you connect with the divine feminine. Labradorite is for strengthening your intuition. Rose quartz is for opening your heart. Moonstone helps you connect with the moon and your intuition. Selenite will help you connect with the goddess within. Do some research and see

what other crystals you can find that might be helpful.

10. Receiving is a feminine quality that has not been nurtured in most women, so we feel uncomfortable receiving. Start by graciously accepting compliments, gifts that you are given, and allowing yourself to be supported. Let your guy open your door for you allow yourself to be nurtured.

11. Female only time. Have girl's night out with your favorite female friends. Go to chick flicks. Dress up and go out to dinner with a group of friends. Have a spa day with your girls. Make this something you do at least once a month.

12. Create a shrine/altar to the Divine Feminine and put things on there that remind you of your feminine nature. Maybe there is a statue of a female deity that you relate to that you can have as a centerpiece. Put flowers on the altar and crystals and photos of you where your feel beautiful. Uses your creativity to make this sacred space for you.

13. Unleash your inner child. Find ways to be playful. Set aside time to play. Be playful, positive, joyful and light as much as possible.

14. Work with the Awakened Feminine meditation cards. Let the images in the Alcyone Rising Meditation Deck help you explore all of the Awakened Feminine parts within you.

The Sacred Marriage

The ultimate goal in this work is to balance the Sacred Masculine and Sacred Feminine within yourself, so that you can come into relationships as a whole and complete being. This book wouldn't be complete without mentioning the Sacred Marriage, at least briefly.

My mission on the planet is to empower people to embrace the Sacred Feminine so you will have to find someone that is doing the Sacred Masculine work and work with them to embrace that part of yourself.

What is the Sacred Marriage?

Each gender holds both masculine and feminine energies within that are beyond gender. Through the process of doing our inner work toward becoming conscious and awake all of the selves that we once were and all the wounds we have suffered get transformed and a new consciousness is born.

The reality is that our longing for love and intimacy with another person can be a powerful motivation for doing the work of creating harmony between our inner masculine and feminine forces. We usually reach that point when we have had a series of relationships that didn't work. We decide we want more and know that we have to work on ourselves before that can happen.

Thus, begins the process of the Sacred Marriage.

I would like to share a profound thing that happened to me that activate the Sacred Marriage for me.

At 4 AM on March 20th, 2016, in the Equinox window, I had a dream. A ritual was performed for me by some angelic beings and the Six-pointed Star and the Vesica Pisces, which both represent the sacred marriage, were placed in my body. The Six-pointed Star was placed in my heart and the Vesica Pisces was place in my Womb/Solar Plexus. The Solar Plexus and the womb are the part of our body where our personal power and creativity live. I woke up from the dream, wrote it down in my journal, noting how powerful it was and went back to sleep.

Twelve hours after that dream I had the first of 5 heart attacks, that lead to me needing open heart surgery. This started an initiation for me into opening my heart and activating the Sacred Marriage.

I knew from the beginning something powerful was about to happen because of the symbolism of that dream. What I didn't know was that I would have a series of heart attacks that spanned two continents, open heart surgery, a relationship with a covert narcissist and the death of my mother, all within 4 years almost to the date. This is a story that fills another book, Resilient Heart.

Each of these events played a big part in healing my heart, opening it up so I could love and ultimately bring balance to my inner masculine and feminine.

By placing the Six-pointed Star in my heart and the Vesica Pisces in my womb/power center the process of the Sacred Marriage was activated. From there I had to do the work to be able to hold the technology of the Awakened Feminine and Awakened Masculine. As you can see, I had a lot of deep work to do to heal my broken heart. It was work I was required to do so that I could be in a conscious, loving relationship with my male counterpart. I had to be whole if I wanted to attract a man who was also whole.

You will see the Vesica Pisces and the Six-Pointed Star in a lot of my paintings.

This is the Vesica Pisces:

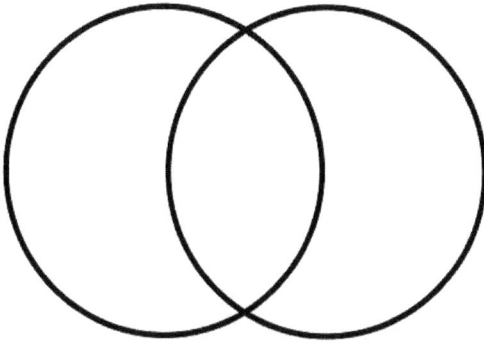

The sacred geometry meaning behind the Vesica Pisces is vast, but it is basically the representation of the union of the Masculine and Feminine and how when they come together, they create a third consciousness. It is a symbol often used to represent the Sacred Marriage. It is the ultimate symbol of creation and manifestation.

The ancient Vesica Pisces (the center of the symbol) is a symbol for the divine femininity, the beginning of new life, gateway to life, the reconciling of opposites, the union of Heaven and Earth.

When the Sacred Marriage takes place within yourself the

feminine and masculine unite to create a more authentic, powerful, creative, loving you. You fall in love with yourself first and from there you can fall in love with someone else.

It is also known as the Universal Womb which births all of creation so, it's profound that it would be placed in my womb.

This is the Six-Pointed Star:

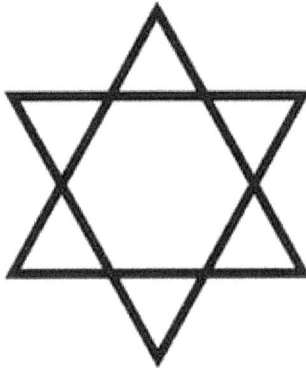

The Six-Pointed Star is an ancient symbol that has a number of meanings. It is known as the Star of David and is much older than Judaism. As an archetypal symbol of the Sacred Union of opposite energies, it's the yin-yang of western civilization.

It is the image of the Sacred Masculine and Sacred

Feminine conjoined as one being. This alchemical symbol of the Union of Male (the upward pointing triangle) and Female (the downward pointing triangle) deconstructs into male and female on the physical plane.

It is formed by the intertwining of the "fire" and "water" triangles (the male blade and female chalice) this symbol represents the masculine and feminine principles in perfect union, the Sacred Marriage or Hieros Gamos. This symbol has long been acknowledged as the model for balance and wholeness.

For me the sacred initiation I took after having the dream about these two symbols was the journey of uniting my power center (masculine) with my heart (feminine).

Many of us are being called to do the inner work of the Sacred Marriage at this time so that we can help lift the consciousness of the planet into union with the Awakened Feminine and Awakened Masculine.

What is presented in Alcyone Rising; the path of the Awakened Feminine is one half of that work. In order to bring back balance and equality for the feminine and females on this planet we each must learn how to embrace our own feminine nature. In concert with that work we must each learn how to embrace our own masculine nature.

Ultimately, the path to successful relationship is part of a larger process that involves restoring harmony and balance between masculine and feminine energies on many levels. This crucial work has been linked in many ancient traditions as the path to establishing world peace. Until we end the gender war within ourselves, there is no possibility for peace between men and women or peace between nations of the world.

When I asked my guides what the meaning of these symbols in my dream were, this is what they told me:

"This is an inner technology. To begin, they are both measurements of the balance between the masculine and feminine within. It is in that balance that you can manifest your desires.

The Heart is the communicator with your soul and the Universe. Your womb is where you bring desire into manifestation.

Both must be in balance. The heart must communicate with your womb, not your brain communicating with your womb." So, it is the heart/womb, Feminine/Masculine connection that helps us manifest what we desire into the world.

When I had the dream the sacred geometry of the Vesica

Pisces and the Six-Pointed Star were actual seeds of remembering that were planet in my body. I had to go through a four-year initiation to remember who I was.

So, I place in your hand the mysteries that I learned through 25+ years of study and experience plus my four-year initiation into the Sacred Marriage of the Awakened Masculine and Awakened Feminine. My focus here being on the Awakened Feminine.

Let this book be your guide and let the images speak for themselves and take you on your own journey to discover and embrace the Awakened Feminine.

About the deck and Katelyn's Paintings:

This deck (sold separately) contains 63 images of the Awakened Feminine that came through visionary artist, Katelyn over a span of 25+ years as she explored her own Awakened Feminine.

Each image contains frequency codes of information that will activate the Awakened Feminine in you as you work with them. There are no words to accompany the images because the frequency codes speak to you at a soul level and say something different to each woman. Words would only pin them down and the Divine

Feminine doesn't want to be presented that way. You are being asked to trust your intuition and soul wisdom to get what you need from each card. You will pick up new information each time you work with the cards.

Through her innate gifts of clairvoyance (seeing visions), claircognizance (knowing what shouldn't be known) and being a channel of etheric intelligence, Katelyn has the gift of being able to paint deeply profound, coded images that transform consciousness.

When you look at one of Katelyn's paintings your soul understands, and your frequency is changed. You don't need to understand what the painting is about, your soul knows, and it changes you.

The paintings are coded frequencies that are Light Language, which is ancient language that we all understand on a cellular level because it comes through your higher self. When you view an image, it activates something deep inside of you. It clears and activates at the same time.

These images are literally out of this world. They are coded with spiritual information that impacts you on a higher level. Trying to understand the message spoils the magic, so just take it in.

Each painting takes a journey of its own creation and tells a unique soul informed story. It is a piece of an unfolding story of evolution and awakening. The images as a whole tell a complete story of the Awaken Feminine.

Each painting is a window into the wisdom of the Universal Heart that created us all. The images that come through Katelyn's clear vision, soul, and hands, creates an energetic field that touches you in a deep way when you view it. They are directives from the universe to my body, mind and spirit to create change and that is why the predict the future. They are like prescriptions.

Working with the Cards:

The cards that you hold in your hands can take you on a journey deep within you and their energy can stimulate healing and open your consciousness to the Awakened

Feminine. It is comforting to find that a thread of continuity connects us all to the past, present, future and ultimately to the Source. The cards are an offering from deep within Katelyn's soul to yours.

Allow yourself to move from your head into your heart so that you can follow the images on your own journey toward healing your inner feminine. Let them act as a window into your inner landscape. Let each image speak to you in your own language; be it art, writing, poetry, dance or movement.

Use the images as an entry point. As you follow the thread of your own inner wisdom let the image itself fall away. Be open to the meanings of any one image as it changes over time. Start an Awakened Feminine journal and follow the patterns that emerge for you for within the patterns lies the true wisdom.

May the images enrich and heal your life, evoke inner wisdom and creativity, bringing you closer to the Awakened Feminine and your connection with the Divine Mother.

There are many ways to work with the cards. Pull one card each day and use it as a meditation piece or a journal portal and let it speak to you. Open to what it has to say. It might say one thing at one time and something else the next time you look at it. Ask the Divine Feminine what She would like to share with you. Or ask how the image relates to your life right now. Come up with your own questions. Have fun with the images and let them inform you.

The Cards as A Meditation Practice

Begin your journey by finding a comfortable place to sit either in a chair or cross legged on the floor. You might also choose the lay on the floor if that feels more comfortable. Close your eyes and breath slowly and deeply counting down from ten to one to come to a place of relaxation.

Continue your breathing as you imagine that there is a star at base of your feet and extending down through the floor and down to the core of the earth. This is your Earth Star. If you wish you can imagine that this is like a root of a tree, growing deep into the ground connecting to Mother Earth who sends you nourishment. Imagine the energy coming up through the Earth and coming into your body and flowing into your heart.

At about 18 inches above your head imagine another star. This is your soul star. Send a cord up into the core of the Universe and receive the energy being sent to you. Imagine that energy moving into your body through your crown and into your heart where it mixes with the energy from Mother Earth. Feel the energy from Mother Earth and Father Sky filling you with their love. You are filled with a sense of peace, relaxation and acceptance.

As you continue to breathe at a slow pace put the deck in your right hand (left hand if you are left handed) and draw the cards up and let them drop back into your hand until a card falls naturally from the deck. This is the card that you will use for your meditation.

Begin to write and draw what comes to you. Think about the color, shapes, symbols, movement or placement of things and what they say to you. What was the first thing that jumped out at you from the image? That might be an important clue to follow. Ask for a message from the card and listen.

Put this card where you can see it and let it inform you as the day goes on. Revisit it before you go to sleep and see what it has to say.

The Awakened Feminine Journal

Start an Awakening Feminine Journal to go deeper into the exploration of the images. Here are some questions you might use in your daily journal to gain insight from the cards. Use them as a way to brainstorm with yourself. Answer the questions quickly and spontaneously so you get your first impressions as a jump off point. Write the first thing that comes to your mind and move on.

- What shapes, symbols, colors stand out to you?
- What energy or feeling would you attribute to this image?

- What do they mean to you?

- Does the woman in the image have anything in her hand? The right hand is the giving hand, the left is the receiving hand. What are you giving or receiving?

- What qualities does she show you?

- What is she thinking, doing, feeling?

- Write a paragraph or so about the information you gathered from the question.

- How can you use this information to help you in your life today?

- How can you integrate what you discovered?

Remember you may get different information from the same card at different times. That is the beauty of this process and not having words for the cards. Have fun with the process and let the Awakened Feminine speak through the cards and through you.

We are the ones we have been waiting for and we will change the world.

IT'S TIME TO LOVE YOURSELF!
I mean, **FIERCELY** love yourself!
By only wanting what is best for you no matter what.

By following your heart

By knowing beyond anyone else's opinion that you
are **AMAZING**.
By **LISTENING** to the song of your soul and following
it.
By saying NO when you feel NO and YES when you
feel YES!

By honoring your body and give it the fuel, nourishment
and movement that it needs.

By honoring all of your feelings

By **LIVING** a balanced life.
By disregarding societies images and standards for
perfection.

By being kind to yourself

By not owning or believing other people's stories about
you.

By surrounding yourself with people who get who you
are and honor you as a gift to the planet.

By not compromising for the sake of acceptance.

By setting boundaries that support you

By understanding that the limitations you feel are being
created by you and let them go.

By knowing that your path is right and perfect just as it is
and there are no mistakes.

By not owning other people's or societies projections

By allowing and opening to all good things to manifest in
your life.

By embracing your courage and just being **YOU!**
By not holding back or censoring yourself and letting
your light **SHINE***
By letting go of people, places and things that no longer

serve you.

By giving yourself permission to be **AUTHENTIC!**
By embracing **FREEDOM**!
By showering yourself with daily doses of **LOVE**.
By eating chocolate if you feel like it.

By giving yourself permission to **SOAR**!
By making a commitment to
live **AUTHENTICALLY,** knowing there is something
only you can bring to the world.
**IT IS TIME TO LOVE YOURSELF FIERCELY!
DO IT NOW...**
Katelyn Mariah

Take in the frequencies of the Awakened Feminine and own it!

We are the ones we have been waiting for and we will change the world.

About Katelyn Mariah

Katelyn is not your ordinary artist. She is a shamanic artist who paints images that transform the viewer.

She is a visionary artist as well as a trained expressive arts therapist with training in art therapy, sandplay therapy and play therapy. She has been an artist since she was a young girl. Katelyn studied fine arts at The Minneapolis College of Art and Design and the University of Minnesota, where she earned a Bachelor of Fine Arts

Degree. She received a master's degree, in Human Development from St. Mary's University in Winona, Minnesota, with an emphasis in Art, Art Therapy, and Child Abuse.

For 26 years Katelyn has pursued both a career in Art and has worked as a psychotherapist. She has been able to use the combined gifts of art and psychotherapy to work with children at risk of abuse and neglect and their families in numerous settings including: emergency shelter, residential treatment programs, a community center in a challenged neighborhood, in schools, as the director of a Therapeutic Preschool, in in-home family therapy and private practice. Katelyn served as the president of The Minnesota Art therapy Association for a two-year term and on the Board of the Minnesota Sandplay Therapy Group for a three-year term.

Katelyn has been exploring the Sacred Feminine through art, writing and her personal work for 25+ years. She is the creator to the Awakening the Goddess Meditation Deck. The images in these cards span 25 years of paintings from the beginning of her journey with the

Sacred Feminine.

Working with Katelyn

Katelyn is available to work individually with people wanting to explore the Awakened Feminine Path on a deeper level, in person and through the internet. She is also facilitating group experiences locally and online. Contact her at by phone at 651-955-3673 or at mystickcreekpublishing@gmail.com

Commission Katelyn for a personal transformational painting.

Katelyn has transformed her own life with painting for over 30 years! Art has been her most transformational path.

Visionary art can show you things that are hidden in your unconscious. Once they are brought to light you can work with and transform them.

One of Katelyn's gifts as a visionary artist is to go to other realms as well as connect with guides and gather information, bring it back and paint it.

What she has done for herself, through visionary art, for 30+ years she can also do for you. Do you have an issue you have been wrestling with that you want to transform, or a desire you would like to bring to fruition? Would you like to explore the Awakened Feminine on a deep personal level?

Put your higher self together with Katelyn's and she will paint a painting for you to work with. This is done on higher realms, so you don't need to be with Katelyn for her to create a painting for you.

Katelyn has 30+ years of unwavering dedication to her craft and her spiritual path that is accessed when she paints. She has a BFA in fine art and has studied with a master painter for 4 years in various countries around the world to learn a Renaissance painting technique.

It's time to find the answer to that question you have been asking!

She has various sizes available to make them affordable for everyone.

Message Katelyn and let's create a vision for you!

Websites:

www.katelynmariahvisionaryartist.com

www.alcyone-rising.com

www.mystickcreekpublishing.com

www.intheheartofthefeminine.com

Email: mystickcreekpublishing@gmail.com